Naked
Truths

Naked Truths

MICAELA MEAD

ARTIVISTIC PRESS

New York

IVI
PRESS

116 West 23rd Street, 5th Floor
New York, NY
10011

First ARTIVISTIC Press paperback edition September 2019

ARTIVISTIC Press can bring authors to your live event. For more information or
to book an event, contact *events@artivisticpress.com* or visit our website at
www.artivisticpress.com/events.

BISAC: POETRY / Subjects & Themes / Love & Erotica. I SELF-HELP / Personal
Growth / General. | BODY, MIND & SPIRIT / General.
LCCN 2019914552 | ISBN 9780578225579

Cover image and design by Micaela Mead

10 9 8 7 6 5 4 3 2 1

for all the lovers and ex-lovers

It's all about love, isn't it?

Contents

PREFACE
It's all about love, isn't it?

This first question is the central theme of everything you will find in the following pages.

However, there were two other questions that kept coming up in the process of writing this book, and I found myself continually asking myself:

What about the pieces of ourselves that we struggle to love?

Whether physical or otherwise… *How can we possibly share them with someone else?*

For me, a large part of the answers to both of those questions lies in individual authenticity.

Personally, it took me a long time to be comfortable enough in my own skin to admit that I was trying way too hard. I was trying to force myself into boxes I could not inhabit. By acknowledging this truth, I made the decision and commitment to no longer accommodate any damaging expectations, even if they were my own. In an instant, I was suddenly free to put all of that energy into caring for myself and others, instead of caring what others thought of me.

"Own your truth." is a common recommendation, but in order to "own" our individual truths, we must be vulnerable… Maybe with others. Most certainly with ourselves.

No matter where you might be on your own journey toward this acceptance, I hope you'll hear me when I say that you are beautiful, attractive, and sexy, just as you are. In your own body. As your most authentic self. Today. Tomorrow. Always.

If you've been waiting for permission or approval, consider this your sign.

Embrace who you are, in all of your glory. Fat rolls, wrinkles, stretch marks, cellulite, emotional baggage, messiness and all.

Because that's the real secret, my love. Your beauty, your true perfection, is in all of your "imperfections".

To be naked is to be vulnerable.

Being naked, without artifice or pretense, invites scrutiny and judgment. But being naked also invites unbelievable connection and pure joy.

Just as authenticity requires vulnerability, vulnerability requires authenticity. In fact, *authenticity is vulnerability*. They are one and the same.

Similarly, there is no individual narrative separate from our collective experience of love and vulnerability. Therefore, *Naked Truths* is not my story. It is your story. It is our collective story.

This is your life.

I hope you have the courage to live it on your own terms.

And if not, perhaps you will find some inspiration somewhere within these pages… a whispered reminder that, in fact, the courage you've needed has been waiting within you all along.

With a kiss of kindness,

xx
Micaela

Naked Truth

DEDICATION

this is for the lovers

the fighters

the ones holding on tighter

than they ever thought

they would

if you've ever loved

if you've ever lost

if you've ever felt you gave more than you got

this is for you

if you've ever looked around and known you could not

climb any higher

even though you're a survivor

it gets pretty cold at the top

and if you've never felt lower

please know that you're not

alone

if you've ever felt lonely

this is for you

for one

for all

I know you don't know me

but is it cliché to say

I've seen your soul in my heartbeat

see, this is me

and this is for you

together

we will keep on existing

persisting

insisting

there's beauty in our damages

if you've ever had your heart broken

this is for you

the ones who

get up when they get cut open

put back together with jagged stitches or glue

we may be ragged and bleeding

but the wounds are misleading

because all of this has been leading me

forward

to you

HOW IT STARTS

this is how it starts

a few words on a page

dark splotches of ink

that sink

and stain

your thoughts in a way

that they'll never be removed again

COOL

I tried to keep my cards close to my chest
when I was looking at you
but my mouth was far too dry
and my hands got all wet with sweat
and I was unable to
I was unstable and unbalanced
and to my dismay
they all fell onto the table
in total disarray
a flush of hearts and heat across my face
ink blots of hot pink on my dimples
my entire agenda in full display
I know I looked like a fool to you
I was sure you could hear
my wild heart in my chest
when you asked how I was
but you played it cool in the way that you do
meanwhile I couldn't decide
if I wanted to crawl away and hide
or recite a sonnet
or maybe burst into song
but I croaked out instead
"I'm okay, how about you?"
I nearly choked when
you leaned in and said in my ear
"wanna get out of here?"
there was only one word in my head

and it was the one that I said
so all that came out was:

"COOL"

DEVIL

catching moonlight on your pillow
shaking stardust in your sheets
some times I seem so sweet
but that's just one side of me

I might have an angel on my shoulder
but I'm the devil in your bed
when you hold me close
I'm set ablaze with sacred smoke

the midnight sun keeps rising
as we're standing in the street
embers burn the soles of our dancing feet
the heat between us grows

now I'm coming undone
and you carry me home
leaving a trail of blazing memories along the road

WHEN I FALL

when I fall, I fall hard
hit the ground running
stunning
roll
but don't go far
foolhardy
charging straight into the fray
do I give myself away?
battered, bruised
I fall to you
and I can't help but wonder
will you be falling, too?
I need to know
will you be there to catch me
when I fall for you?

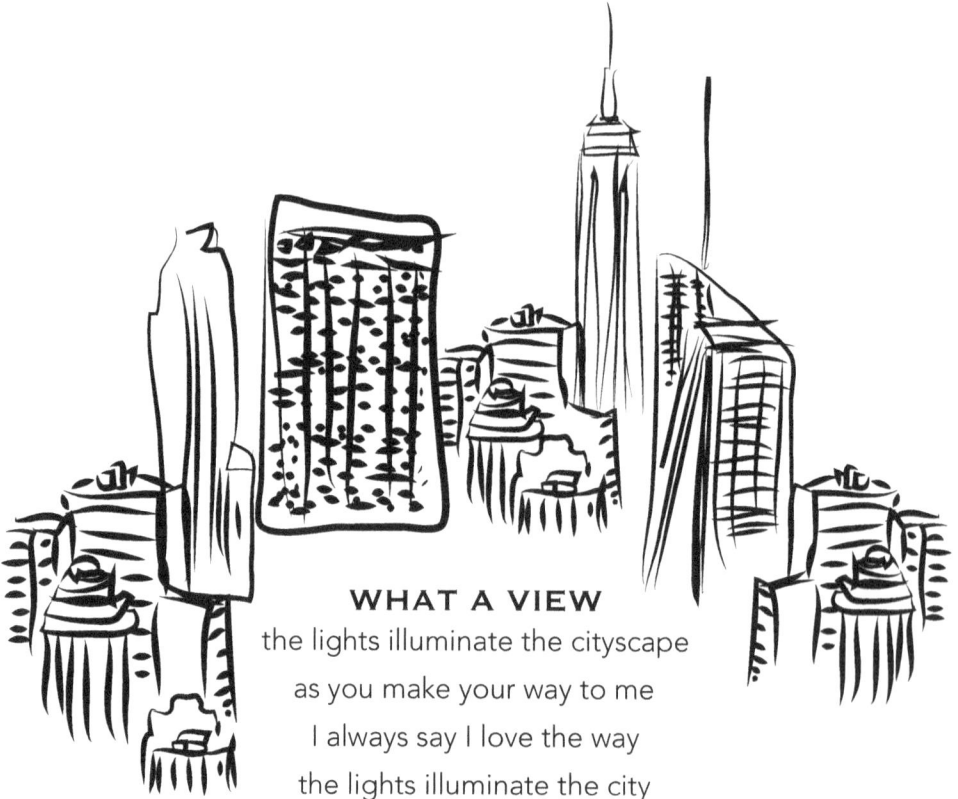

WHAT A VIEW

the lights illuminate the cityscape

as you make your way to me

I always say I love the way

the lights illuminate the city

and while the skyline in your eyes

is truly so brilliant to see

the prettiest view

is my view of you

PAPAYA

you're prettier than a papaya colored sunrise

and I'd rather not witness a glorious sunset

than miss

the sweetness of your kiss

or never dive into the deep, uncharted bliss

which resides

in the depths of your eyes

#LOVENOTES

I love that you pick up pennies
I love that you spruce up the flowers you send me
incandescent happiness and joy never ending…
or so the story goes
I love your wispy bits of hair
I love the countless memories we share
the innumerable ways you choose to enumerate
you care
I'll always keep you close

and when you're feelin' low
you can let me know
and I'll do my best to make it better
send you a love note
or a hidden quote
or a smile hid in a letter
just let me know
and I will show
from your head down to your toes
you're the best made even better

I love what you love
and that you love me
you're perfection in truth and form
I love how you love
I love how you get me
you're the one they wrote the standards for

the wrinkles in your smile
the freckles on your nose
the crinkles at your eyes
the way your features glow
I love the way you love me
I'll always keep you close

WONDER

your body is a wonderland

someone said

yours is

far from convention's design of perfection

and yet

with my mind's eye I spy divine in your thighs

and in the things society says you should hide

I find myself

trapped inside your enraptured sighs

I get lost in the way

you breathe

THE WAY I SEE IT
we'll both live forever or die together

that's the only way it can be

INK

black lines on your wrists
I want to sink into
your eyes
our minds aligned
can I trace the signs on your skin
and let the fire burn out from within
charged, charred, black
beautiful, saturated moments where
you draw patterns on my thighs
and sign your name on my side
writing the language of my sighs
in nighttime hues: blues
infused with the two of us
touching your skin
tracing the lines of ink
I'd like to tattoo my name across your heart
my body is a book of blank pages
for you to fill
with your compositions
hold my hand in place
and I'll hold your heart
in the space of moments
minutes
breaths
forever can be torn apart
you draw me back
but the drawback is your attack

now we're drawing lines of blood
in angry red
erasing ties
drawing lines in the sand
and writing lines instead
to convey our goodbyes
this euphoric happiness
was an explosion of light
a constellation of forsaken stars
in the darkness
my heart is an overflowing sink
permeated with the same black ink
you used to
paint my skin
with your midnight kisses
I wish I could follow the lines
one more time
but this sadness has such a beautiful cadence

LONG NIGHTS

the night leaves moonlight on your skin
sunlight seeps softly through the shades
for a heavenly eternity we lay
fingers interlaced

you take and take, but for you I'd give it all away

long nights fade into days
now there's sunlight peeking through the shades
leaking in to illuminate the empty space
where the shape of you used to lay

long nights fade into days
now there's moonlight in your place
so I drink it in
but some things can't be replaced

the quicksilver paint of pain illuminates our mistakes
like a silver blade sinking into the space
between my ribs
there's no remedy for this ache

some things just can't be replaced

long nights fade into days
and I know there's so much that I can't say
but at least the words I wrote upon your skin

will never fade

ECLIPSE

my mind's a mess right now
I really don't know how
to make sense of any of this
it's all about love, isn't it?
this is unfamiliar territory
thought I'd traversed it all before
thought we shared the same story
but now I'm not sure
don't get comfortable
everything changes
the past morphs and rearranges
ink on skin and blood on pages
the rhyme sinks in
slow depression moves in stages
once you get comfortable, everything changes
this is unfamiliar territory
thought I'd traversed it all before
thought we shared the same story
but now I'm not sure
no, now I'm waiting for my feelings
to eclipse me
I've never wanted anything
so much
try so hard, can't give you up
I'm waiting for my feelings to eclipse me
I've never wanted anything so much

LOSING SLEEP

you're like the moon
and I keep losing sleep
howling at you

every night I lie wide awake
staring up at your face
amidst the stars
a beacon in the expanse of heartless darkness
but your heart isn't beating next to mine
my memories do their best to
mimic its absent heat
but the absence of its beat
is beating me up
and the opal glow of things I don't know
and can't control
becomes harsh with its hardness

you're like the moon
and when I can't sleep
I repeatedly lose my sleep and sanity
imagining your glow is home

I'm like a moth to your flame
drawn to your light
though it burns me up
from inside
at least you chase the shadows

from my mind

you're like the moon
and I keep howling at you
repeatedly losing sleep and sanity
imagining you're with me

but at least you chase the shadows
from my mind

LINGER

come to me.
linger.
tricking my racing heart
you don't see
hush.
I know.

finger
lacing blood with fire.
let the heat
grow
flushed
you, me. one.

bigger.
ticking bomb in chest.
words in a
rush
flow
one, two, three.

vigor
facing the impossible end.
and then we
slow.
blush.
you, me, done.

one to three

figures

licking, like a breath

you let me

just

go.

A DEPARTURE

and once the hall was blessed

he left

feeling satisfied.

HOW TO LOSE SOMEONE
IN TEN WORDS OR LESS:

"I think that maybe, possibly, I'm in love with you"

"I think I may be in love with you…"

"I think I'm possibly in love with you"

"I think I'm in love with you"

"I think I may love you"

"I think I love you"

"I might love you"

"I love you…"

"love me"

"I…"

I say, watching your eyes widen

narrow

and disappear from my view

as you blink rapidly in a series of short lines of morse

S.O.S.

I laugh

it's the only thing I can do

or else I'll cry

it's so painfully obvious

you don't feel the same

when you say you need some time

I nod slowly

trying to appear nonchalant

but when you walk away

I'm certain I've already lost you

IT TAKES TWO

listen carefully

it takes two

to tangle

twisted hearts and broken parts

thorns and scars

fetters, bars

like a train on tilted tracks

you never see it coming.

sea foam to pool to Niagara Falls

to scorching desert

deserted

when did this idyllic dirt road become hot lava?

like putting out a forest fire with a dewdrop

SMOKE

if you could read my mind, would you like how you feel?

'cause I don't

if you could see inside, would you know what is real?

'cause I don't

and I don't even know if there is anything left for me to say

should we just walk away?

does it really matter what we choose to do

from day to day

if this goes up in smoke?

SHOTS FIRED

if you take your shot

you might regret it

and you can't go back

can't retrace your steps

or pretend you never said it

THE OTHER LINE

I think we forgot how to make our own decisions
and let others pave our way
but distancing becomes division
and eventually it breaks

maybe we forgot how to make our own decisions
and let others pave our way
but baby we can still make what we envisioned
cast the anchor overboard
or else let's just sail away

did you forget how you used to release your inhibitions
when I'm around, your guard comes down
you throw your cares away
but it didn't go that way today
I know I didn't envision what you came to say

I hear you breathing
baby, please stay on the other line
you say you're leaving
but you say that all the time

this love's misleading
I know we've messed it up this time
but of the thousand times I asked you to stay
I'm still watching you walk away

COME ROUND

I still don't understand
why it was you couldn't stay
or how you could go ahead and say
those things you said about me
I guess you're fine
without me
and that hurts more that it did before
I heard your footsteps on the floor
and I swear it sounded as if you ran
though I know you tiptoed out the door
no, I'm not lying
battered on the floor
I'm just sadder than before
because even though you can
you don't come round anymore

ONLY LOVE

you taste like her lips
when you kiss mine
it's all in your kiss
you cannot hide

I know it
you know it too
so what am I to do?

it's hard to admit
but you cannot lie
you owe me this
so just tell me this time

what am I to you?

microphones magnify wild moans
my emptiness is amplified
empty homes and dial tones
full of loneliness inside

you taste like new lips
when you kiss mine
I can't forget this
but you won't see me cry

after all you've put me through

and all that we've been through
tell me, what am I to you?
what am I to do?

it's okay, it's only love
you might say it's only love
but tell me, is love enough?

LIES

no matter how I might search or try
I cannot find the words to describe
how bad it hurt that night
when I finally realized
you lied
and began accepting all the truths that I'd denied
for so long
I wanted
to find someplace to hide
a sturdy shield to stay behind
or a wall to guard this heart of mine
because
I'm no longer safe with you
unwanted
obviously
but I felt haunted
by the things you left behind
spoiled memories
other things I couldn't see
all these scars of ours became my jewelry
festering, diseased, pestering me endlessly
shackled to the idea that I will never be free
I can never leave
even though you made it look so easy
repeating
that
there is nothing I can do

to bring you back to me

but the past
is past
you're not coming back
and I imagine that
after all we've been through
I wouldn't want you to

at least
that is what I can say to you
and bite my tongue as I do
to prove that

I know how to lie, too

RIPPED

and then she packed her bags
and took all she got from me
I said "you know I didn't mean it…"
she said "you know that I'm still leaving"
and when she saw me cry
she just pointed at your ripped jeans

you know I didn't mean it
but I still cheated

and there's no repairing this
this time

TO DRAW BREATH

I write poetry like you breathe air
the words are a never ending rhyme:
not even there

ask me what you may and I'll put it to verse…
make some simplified perfect image
to cast all that hurts
a twisted thorn
a barb in your side
one single drop of blood on the page
to symbolize the wounds I hide
you see, I might've lost myself
but I have no need to be found
I'm crippled here as I stare you down
can you feel my gaze
like razor blades
or a silken touch
that hurts just as much
these words of yours are a curse of mine
a never ending circuit
running my mind
and cutting me up

SHATTERED

love is large, a gaping hole in my heart

one to two and two to one to nothing

everything flies dynamically apart

icy slopes leave you trapped

in a cold glass of silence

mingling with hot alcohol and trying not to shatter

HEART

the heart
is a flimsy thing
it breaks over nothing.

BOOKENDED

you can't outrun the memories
or run to something you cannot find
so I'm stuck here lost in reverie
hoping that might change
in time

my mind's a sieve which has me trapped
grain by grain, the hours slip past
but there's a crack in the glass
if I could slip through, can we get the time back?

you were just the same
like all the rest but with a different name
I keep hoping that might change
in time…
but it doesn't work like that

the words in my throat always make me choke
I know
if I could just get them out, I could run to hope…
but just like bile they catch and hold
I don't know what to do

my narrowed options are down to two:
run to safety
or stay with you

it's true
you can't outrun the memories
or run to something you cannot find
so I'm stuck here lost in reverie
hoping that might change
in time

WISH YOU WERE HERE

I wanted to put down in pages
all these thoughts
of chaos within the chaos of my head…
but the moment I sat down
and the moment I set down
my pen against the page
the chaos dissipated
and my chaotic brain went dead
oh where are you now
thoughts, heart, you?
where'd you go?
where next might you head to?
wherever you are
and wherever you go
I hope it's nice
I hope the weather's fine
drop a line
or send a postcard
if you decide
you might stop by
sometime

THE WRECK

he fills the cracks and spaces

left by all your ever-changing faces

you leave me hanging

he takes me places

you wither in comparison to all his graces

but whatever thing he cannot do

I find me searching for in you

and I find me searching him for shades of you

you're the features I always see

and though there are more things to like

between the likes of him and me

the things alike between you and me

are more alike than he and I will ever be

when I rearrange the pieces

I wonder how this could ever be…

but I simply can't give up our legacy

the raggedly perfect imperfection

of the wreck of you and me

VIRUS

I've become complacent
about erasing your memory
you always meant a lot to me
so somehow I cannot compute
how you turned into
the enemy
now you open windows
to my past
when I don't want you to
and my disk is full of folders
of tracks I'll never send
a prosperous beginning
which ended up burning
and turned into the end
the story of an enemy
who started as a friend
and I can't get through to you
no way to sort the old from new
I'm infected
your virus has taken root and taken hold
you've saturated every cell
and obliterated everything else
I can't decode the ultimate truth
and I can't get rid of you
so you just continue to open windows to my past
when I don't want you to

HOME

home can be a space
or a face or a resting place
but now none of that is true
you left no trace when you went away
and I
I'm straddling the borderline of the undefined
without you

now I'm
airing out these empty rooms
and watching the dust blooms
without you
even the dust blooms
without you

I wish I could say I miss you
I just miss the things we used to do
I wish we could go back to me and you
'cause I liked the me I was with you
but you don't feel like home anymore

you have a key
but you can leave it with me
'cause you don't feel like home anymore
it's not that things went wrong
I've just been gone too long
and you don't feel like home anymore

LOOKING BACK

in the future
will we look back on today
and say
where did it all go wrong?
will we be able to see things start to change
or fall apart?
what will be left behind by the raging fires we hold
collectively in our hearts?
nothing lasts
will we live to see the flames of humanity
eventually die out
char our organs
and turn us to ash?
particles of us float about in the past
the past, like the future, is eternal smoke
slipping through our fingers
its scent lingers
hanging in mind
like the kind of scent you find
in a place where things and memories go to die
ashes to ashes, dust to dust
all of this will go up in bright red flames
like bleeding rust
around the hinges of our corroded, corrupted lives
because when there is no fraction of kindness left
there will be no fraction of sanity left
and that will be the end of things

new, uncertain ways of living
are what the unexpected future brings
and in looking back
we'll surely see how
looking back changes everything

KNEW YOU

your truth is different than mine, that's fine
just make sure you can still find you
in all the lies
or despite what you may do
your truth may be different than mine
but make sure you can still find you
because I can't tell you
who the hell
that is

SPACE

I need to clear a space
for all my anxious thoughts
inside this messed up mind of mine
honestly, I feel betrayed
and maybe a little bit played
I thought maybe you were what I prayed for
but now I'm stuck here waiting
waiting
I still feel a bit betrayed
but I'm stuck here waiting
hoping you would say more
but you don't say anything

SETTLE DOWN
it's times like these
where I'd love to
settle down
yet I pack up and leave
and
inevitably
get the hell out
of this town

NEW YORK IS OVER

you said
"New York is over
and getting colder
full of people I don't know
I'm getting older
ain't got no place to go
but this city's getting old"

truth be told
New York was good before ya
but now it's over
yeah, New York was good before ya
but now it's over
so I said
"Toronto… Nashville… Atlanta…
Georgia could be good for ya
Chicago, Austin, are waiting for ya
I think you oughta go"

maybe you should move to California
where the streets are paved with gold
some sunshine might be good for ya
a change of pace, you know?
       if you go and move to California
            maybe you won't be so cold

WHEN THERE'S NOTHING ELSE

what the hell, we could have made it

FOREVER WOULDN'T WAIT

forever wouldn't wait for us. we held on hard to its coattails, but winced as the last ragged shreds of our familiar fantasy slipped through our fingers. the bitter taste of mediocrity and disappointment tickled our tongues and scalded our throats, a lasting reminder of the things that we lost, which, it turns out… we'd never even had to begin with.

CHANGES

I didn't think you'd listen
didn't think you'd stay
didn't wanna give in
or give it all away
I told you that
I told you it would change

I'm staring at the light now
I know we said goodnight now
but I don't want to go out
thinking how we could've made this right
we can make this right now
I don't wanna fight now
but you just pick a side
and it isn't mine
how?
how can you say those words to my face
take a breath and just breathe, it's okay
no it's not, and you know that's a joke
but you hope
and I pray, I pray the words that you dare to say
it's not okay, but it will all be okay someday

I didn't think you'd listen
didn't think you'd stay
didn't wanna give in
or give it all away

I told you that
I told you it would change

but will it be for the worse or better?
that I cannot say

FORGOTTEN ARTS

I'm erasing the remnants of me and you, and all we knew

but there's a part of you and me that I can't forget

clarity is hard to see

there's an art to being renewed that I don't quite get

yes, clarity is hard to see

this will be hard to fix

there's an art to forgetting and letting go

that I don't know

yet

EMPTY GLASS

you tear me apart, but I still miss you
you've broken my heart, but I still wanna kiss you
you've shunned me
stunned me
and completely undone me, yeah
but I still want you
need you
am desperate to keep you

and it's like I crave your chaos
I want your cruelest touch
if I ask you for your everything
do I ask of you too much?

yeah, it's funny, but I still miss you
like a bottle of whiskey I don't wanna get through
wanna savor your flavor
though it burns going down
yeah, I still want you
need you
am desperate to keep you around

it's like I crave your chaos
and I want your cruelest touch
if I ask you for your everything
do I ask of you too much?

of course
the emptiness never answers me
and the substance of my memories
never comes back
so I will
build a wall around my heart of glass
and watch the past refract

MESSY

love is messy

trust me

I'm sure

I could be the one you leave her for

or you could be the one

he's leaving me

for

LOVE IS

love is patient, love is kind
love is hasty, love is blind
do I ever cross your mind?
love is warm and love is gentle
love is way too sentimental
yeah I'll ask you one more time
do I ever cross your mind?
you find mine all the time

do you know what love is?
is it harder than you thought?
do you know what love is?
I can tell you what it's not
it's not going out and getting wasted
or driving home and getting caught
it's slightly stupid
and highly foolish
selfish
but selfless too
it's stupid
how I can't
help myself
to keep from loving you

love is complex, love is simple
it hides in a smile or a dimple
it's the thing you hope you'll find

and it happens all the time
love is hard and love is easy
if you know, then you'll believe me
but if I ask you one more time
will you say I cross your mind?

MAYBE I WAS BLIND
maybe I was blind
but I was willing
I was so captivated by your glint and gleam
that I didn't seem
to see or mind the telltale lies and warning signs
my eyes and mind held hostage by
the breath of lust and sorely misguided trust
which kept me warm for a while

maybe I was blind
but I was willing
maybe I was too busy trying to get your love
or gain your trust
I didn't read the telltale signs of danger's lies
I never dreamed I'd be accosted by
the death of us
like a dulled mirage reduced to dust
I missed the truth in your disguise

maybe I was blind
but I was willing
I didn't see the villain hiding in between
the edges of your smile

DRUNK

let's get drunk and remember
let's get drunk and forget
all I know is
I don't want to be alone in my head
it's so cold when I'm alone in bed
let's get drunk so I can pretend
I'm not alone again
all I know is
I don't want to be alone
it's so cold when I'm alone
and all the old loneliness creeps back in again

MISS COMMUNICATION

I keep thinking you'll call me as the night goes on

but it's getting late

and you know I won't come over just to stay till dawn

you tell me we're just friends

but this feels like something more

is that the kind of friend you take me for?

you say such sweet things

then go and leave me

making sense of what you didn't say

am I your friend or lover or just some other

you left hanging on the line

or can't you make up your mind?

it's getting late and I can't stay

is that the kind of friend you take me for?

either way

it's getting late

and I can't stay

I've been through this shit before

PLAYING GAMES

it gets so hard playing games with half the pieces

I know they never said this would be easy

but I thought it would be easier than this

I'm fighting my way out of a familiar corner

while you're trying to break in

feels like we're playing a game

but there's no way to win

how do I make you realize

it's causing me pain again

I try my best to let you know

but there's no way to show

the scars that broke through

black and blue

again

why does it feel like

your watchful eye

marks every line

playing mind games

with a pen

REAL LOVE
am I enough for you?
you make me feel so see-through
I feel inadequate
even when I'm almost there, you're telling me to quit
it's like we're on a different wavelength
or at least a different page
no matter how loud I shout, you drown me out
and don't hear a thing I say

and I'm uncertain
do you know you're hurting me again
is it worth it?
wish I could tell you how this ends
I just want a loving hand to hold
but you'd rather pick me apart
what's the greatest lie you've told?
I've known this from the start
it changes nothing in the end

I used to be content meeting you where you're at
but lately I don't know if I can keep up with that
it's like we're on a different wavelength
or at least a different page
I keep shouting till I'm hoarse
but of course, you don't hear a thing I say

is this tough for you?

because you make it look so easy
breaking all of this
and taking down all of my defenses
you'd leave me
senseless
like there's nothing much to it
I'd ask for your opinion
but I know what you would say
you tell me every day

and I'm uncertain
you must know you're hurting me again
is it worth it?
I wish I could tell you how this ends
I just want a loving hand to hold
but you'd rather pick me apart
what's the greatest lie you've told?
I've known this from the start
it changes nothing in the end

I guess it's up to you
if you still want to see me
I just don't understand
how you could shun me so completely
when I was injured at your hand
three two one and we're undone
like those moments never mattered
looking back at our broken past

and the innocence you shattered

and now I'm certain
so I'll tell you how this ends
I know I'm worthy
should you try to make amends
I'm not another hand to hold
I should have told you from the start
taking back all you stole
can't heal my heart
so this means nothing in the end

BLOOD STAINS

hot blood, running through my fingers

it comes off, but you know the smell

it lingers

don't you see

this was never about you and me

but I can't help but think of all the things

and wonder at the pain they bring

maybe the shame of your name is my destiny

CARDIABSENT

I'm sure

you must be

my most powerful muscle

my prize

you give so much

sometimes

your strength surprises me

somehow, you always endure

and yet, I realize

you're all alone down there

is that why you feel so weak?

starved for attention

seeking affection

I'm sorry you feel so weak

tell me, dear heart

is it something to do with me?

a lack of empathy?

a deficiency?

hello? heart?

can you hear me?

in the labyrinth of my veins, your pulse barely sounds

"I'm here" you say

but I can barely hear you

are you hiding?

I can't find you

you must be somewhere

forsaken in a dark corner

persisting

or caged in some cavity

resisting

but I can't feel you

why can't I feel you

when I place my hand

squarely over my breast

just here?

I spread my fingers

palm open

senses seeking

trying to open my chest

to find you, its treasure…

70

and all I feel is

nothing

nothing

but a pervading

sense of

fear

no growl

not even a purr

emptiness fills me

replacing

the blood

you circulate

in response, you start racing, pacing

slow and steady, below the ground, your rhythm begins to pound

steady and slow, above the ground seeking down below, I finally feel your sound

are you yet alive, my ferocious heart? still beating? or have you taken every hit you can?

"you are mistaken" you reply, "I have hardly lost my will to live…

I've not endured any measure of excessive displeasure, I've simply given all I have to give"

you once again retreat to your solemn shadows

slinking back into your dark cave

that smells sweet like raw meat

I still feel your heat

but the chill grows

and my blood

slightly slows

left again

without

a

beat

.

.

.

THE EDGE
pictures
are all I have.

and I can't help
your face.
picturing

    picturing

    you,
    me,
    us together.
    thinking

things might be different
if this
was more than it is…

but that's all they are,
pictures.
pictures

    of you,
    of me,
    of us together.

forever?
forever.

forever.
forever?
never.

I hate these pictures

    of you,
    with her.

the image of you two together.

fissures in my state of ecstasy
of you and me.
who is she?
she's not me.
images plastered
against my skull.
too full.   it's all
fractured forever.
I need time to heal.
I feel   too much.
snap. flash. whiplash.
backlash.
love and agony
have never felt more real.

and now   I'm
nothing more than
a silent witness to your private kiss,   sinking,
                                       drowning
in our spoiled happiness,
watching my own happiness   withering away.

I'm locked in   my own fantasy
a nightmare
made from a dream.   now
nothing more than the   spoiled

milk drawn from curdled cream.
impulses flattered
shutters fluttered.
images shattered   by
one single blow.
but we can move on,
can't we?
continue in this state of   ecstasy…
turn a torn corner
and continue anew
this fractured-mirror union
of me and you?

grab a corner of the glass
around my heart
and cut your finger to make
the pain
last.
each splinter of   glass reflects
these frozen images
that don't pass
and the pain
becomes an endless refrain
that I hear again and again.   but
nothing changes. the pain   doesn't
fade. I swore I'd   protect
myself this time.

because,
as I grow older I find
fairy tales
are the stories you make up in your mind.
reality has edges:
teeth
or shards of glass
that rip into the heart,   my heart.
when the body's most vital organ   is
violated, it becomes   vulnerable.
in real life,
fairy tales don't always have
happy endings.

that's all they are,
pictures,   images…
but now, somehow
these pictures   are all I have.

A CLOSENESS

maybe my heart is more vulnerable than the rest

but all I know is the way it felt

to be nestled against your chest

my head resting

in the perfectly fit

cradle

of your neck

A RESOLUTION
I don't need this bullshit.

I THINK TOO MUCH.

I think too much
and all these words and thoughts come out
when you're not around
I can't slow them down
but I know I'll be okay
one day I'll be okay
yeah, it'll all be okay
one day

ONE DAY

you've just gotta make it

one more day

don't worry about

the hours

the days

the weeks

the months the years

if a seed falls amidst a forest of pain

it falls upon un-sensing ears

and nobody hears

so let the seed land in the ash of your past

and know that

nothing can be if everything lasts

leave that planted seed be

to grow into a tree

which will climb to declare

a mighty forest thrives here

if you just get through the rest of today

MADDY KAY

sometimes I think about you
the way life feels without you
there are times I think I'm getting better, better, better
but I've never been a good forgetter

I hope you know that I still miss you
and I miss the way it felt to be with you
I want you to know
I don't blame you for wanting to go
I just wish you had let me know

now you're somewhere else, aren't you?
Arizona, L.A., Milan
sometimes this nostalgia hits me hard
till I recall you're really gone

I still miss you
I miss the way it felt to be with you
and I want you to know
I don't blame you for letting go
I just miss you even so

moving on
is hard to do
everyone and everyone else wants me to
but you
you find more moments to pour your presence into

and I still miss the way it felt to be with you

admit to yourself that you were an idiot to not have seen this coming. and that's okay. take a deep breath. don't lie to yourself; it's **not** all "going to be OK". it's just not. and that's okay, too. but just because two things are okay, doesn't mean everything else is. you know that. so take another deep breath and put the lid on the box of things that marked another time in your life. the pieces of the puzzle that made you who you were don't fit together anymore, but those pieces don't equate to who you are. you're not the same anymore. so place the lid on the box, a barrier between you and the past, and hide the box in a closet. or put it out for the garbage man to pick up. burn it. throw it off a cliff or mountain if you live in a location where this is possible. you'll be amazed at how liberating this will be. if you have no cliffs, toss the box out the window of your car. it's not heavy. memories are weightless unless they are inside of you. the box itself is mostly filled with pictures, many many photographs. you don't need them anymore. stop telling yourself you do. he wasn't what you wanted. her absence is what you need. being alone isn't so bad. it's actually very freeing. tell yourself these things. tell yourself these things until you make them true. tell yourself these things until you actually believe them. it's going to hurt for a while, expect that. you **do** expect that. but you don't know just **how much** it's going to hurt. this terrifies you. let this fear and pain fill you up until it becomes an endless oasis, a whirlpool of consuming darkness and sadness and emptiness. and exhale. this single sentence in a chapter of your life does not write your whole story. turn the page, but only one. no matter how much you may wish you could skip ahead, you cannot. buy junk food and tissues and watch sad movies and do nothing and cry and cuddle your kitten your dog your teddy-bear or anyone who will tolerate you. men cry too. even the strongest mountains break, all rocks split and crumble. we all shed tears now and again. allow yourself to cry. allow yourself to feel. after a while you will sense the clouds beginning to clear. don't be fooled. the hurt and the hopelessness will catch you off-guard. be ready. be vigilant. be kind. most of all, be kind to yourself. it's a long and tedious process that cannot be expedited. but the day will come when the clouds do part. it won't be all at once. one day you will notice a ray of sunlight peeking out and spreading over your skin in the shape of a tentative smile. slowly, you will live again. you will learn to define your own happiness on your own terms, and that is when you will realize how far you've come. you might get a dog, smile at a cute girl, buy your mother a present, invest in a spa treatment, laugh at families with babies, or take a trip by yourself. slowly you will emerge. people will comment on how great you look and you will smile sagely. tell yourself you are OK.

you will finally believe it.

and when you look back at the distance you've traversed,
you might even manage to convince yourself you don't
notice
              the trail
                        of
               pictures
              and
                 memories
                        blowing
                                      in
                 the wind.

MAKE IT UP

make it all up.
fashion your stories
your façade
out of nothingness

and start again.

TRUTH

here's the truth:
we're all just struggling
to get through
another day
another month
another year
wondering if
and when
this or that or
we might disappear
if you ask me
we're all juggling work and romance
searching for truth
wanting nothing more
than to be understood…
but we'll settle for less unsure
some of us seek our truth from above
but there's truth down here as well
there's a simple truth
you don't have to seek
in heaven or in hell
that so many don't hear or know:
love is the rain
that dissolves all pain
and makes the flowers grow

ALCHEMICAL REACTION

you go your way and I'll go mine
we meet in the middle every time
making something out of nothing

SUNSET VIGNETTE

as the sky slowly turns its rosy hue
I'm thinking of you
still thinking of you

yeah, I'm a beautiful illusion
diffusing
as night descends

this one's for you

LONELY

I know you're lonely,
but I'm lonely too
my heart's been
reaching out
and bleeding
aching
breaking
calling for you
I know you're lonely
but I've been lonely too
I'll come find you if you say you want me to
I promise I will find you no matter what I do

FEATHERS
it's all caving in
we're all falling down
no one warned us of the softness
as we hit the ground

CREDO

despite how many times

I may get knocked aside

love is my religion

I get up every time

love is my religion

the world is my church

I worship every day

through the testament of my life

FIXER UPPER

maybe a fresh coat of paint is all it will take
to restore this shell to life
but there's more going on that we can't see
the damages dwell inside
you feel the words they throw
like stones through your broken windows
you might look good on the outside
but you're falling apart

if you're hurt, just say so
I know this can be so hard
you might look good on the outside
but you're falling apart

shabby carpet, boarded windows
the damage clearly shows
you're on the market
but you're a fixer upper
baby you're a fixer upper

so many years of wear and tear
you hide your tears but the scars are there
and I'm sorry
babe, I'm so sorry

all that's been done to you
is not what you deserve

but I'm not out to heal a heart
I don't want a fixer upper

maybe I can save more hurt if I do this first
I don't wanna leave you in the dark
but the responsibility is killing me
I can't heal your broken heart
and I'm sorry
babe, I'm so sorry
you might look good on the outside
but you're falling apart

WHAT YOU DESERVE

you deserve long drawn baths
and a lingering gaze
hot nights
balanced by blissful days
and you deserve to be told again and again
what your heart yearns to hear
and your mind guesses at
that you're like the universe
in fact, you light the universe
the stars would fall at your feet to fashion your crown
you deserve so much more than I could ever convey
you brighten the world just by being around
I wish that I could give you all you deserve
but I'm a mere mortal
and the things that you search for
are not of this world

UNFINISHED

you know time flies, keeps going on
but nothing changes
till everything changes
and everything comes undone

but babe, we're not done here
don't give up before we're through
there's something unfinished here
tell me you don't feel it, too
we keep coming back, year after year
you know I'll always come back to you

we did the best we can
now I have to leave
but I'll be back again
ain't seen the last of me

oh, I'm your biggest fan
it's easy enough to see
I always come back again
couldn't ever lose track of me

and in your eyes, I see things undone
but you keep on chasin'
till what you chase
is something you've become
just keep your head down till the work is done

babe, you're not done here
don't give up before it's through
there's something unfinished here
tell me you don't feel it, too

no, we're not done here
don't give up before we're through
there's something unfinished here
tell me you don't feel it, too
we keep coming back, year after year
you know I'll always come back to you

ONE MINUTE

I want to be sure
I'm doing the right thing
giving up and giving in
preparing to take another swing
am I doing the right thing?
I want to be sure
giving up and giving in
as I push my doubt over

I've lost sight of who he was
now I'm discovering who you are
in this game of lies and alibis
no one gets very far

but I'm not lying anymore
not now and not again
things are different than before
and this doesn't have to end
will it? I'm not sure
but for now at least we're
fine
we may not have forever
but we can be together for a minute
or more in time

PAST LIFE

I said I don't believe in magic
that I left those fairy tales far behind
but all those facts are fading
with you in my line of sight
I don't even know how we got to this place
but I can't get you off my mind
no, I never wanted fancy
didn't ask for fame
but the way you're looking at me
it's like you already know my name
now we're inhabiting this space
like our fates are intertwined
I see eternity in your face
like the stars have all aligned
and I've got this feeling that I cannot place
I can't get you off my mind
the room is dark
but it's like you're made of starlight
guiding me into the night
the blackness has never looked so bright
and I've got this feeling that I cannot place
it's like I met you in a past life
and there's no leaving you behind
maybe I followed a path your fingers traced
or met you on a different, distant shore of time
it's like we've been here before
before this moment began

and even if we have, I've never been more sure
I'd do it over and over again

NATURAL

I want you with an intensity that startles my soul
like nature shaking the branches of trees
or splitting the sky with intention
my heart is the parched ground which thirsts for rain
or snow
any kind of precipitation
let your wave break upon my shores
brand your name on my lips
search my corners and my jagged edges
pour fire into my veins and breathe life into my lungs
gasping for air like it's you that I breathe
when you have gone
not even the wind can stir me
when you have gone
there are only embers left
smoldering warmly, bright
but slowly dying
waiting for the lightning to strike
and reignite
bring love back to my life and enliven my soul

LANDMARKS OF ANOTHER LIFE

I went to a bar for a change of scenery

and that's where you inevitably found me

I caught your name in a dream

and it's been haunting me

now we're face to face

and I can't place

the way you look at me

but it feels familiar to me

like I saw your face in a dream

and now it's all I want to see

you and your cut knuckles

me and my ripped jeans

your hand looks like it might be designed

to rest aligned with my face or side

and fit with mine

so perfectly

I grab it as we leave

and you stare at me with a word on your lips

like you really, truly know what it means

so show me

your busted up belt buckle

scrapes my graceless knuckles

and you chuckle

lowly, your fingers slowly lifting

hitching

stitching my heart together with yours

my shirt crumples on the floor

like a paper cup filled with glitter stuff
pouring
the constellation of marks on your skin is familiar to me
like a map or trajectory that only I can see
from where the years and my fingerprints have been
are these remnants of another life we led
or just the ashes of our separate pasts?
we may never know

ALL IN

they say every story's already been written

every love song's already been sung

so why bother tossing my words into the ring

if everything's already been sufficiently done?

if every song's been written and every story told

the truth is

we're all looking for a hand to hold

I don't want another second

to waste another minute

praying, second-guessing

just want to be all in it

I just want your love to fill my soul

SPRAWLING

I'm stuck on your staccato sentences
tripping and falling over your lines
they might be well practiced and refined
but regardless, I'm guard-less
and I find the depths within your irises
send me

s
    p
       r
         a
       w
      l
        i
        n
      g
      every time

WITHIN

I want to climb out of my skin

and try on yours for size

just so I can know

what goes on inside your mind

EARNEST

I thought I loved you before
and I said so
I meant it
and yet I'm amazed at how little I knew
and how much my love grew
I could say I love you best now
but seeing as my love grew then
what's to say it won't again?
I love you much but know
my love has room still left to grow

IF YOU STAY

if you stay
I can't promise I won't change
because I'm growing every day
but I will say
you're the only one
no one else makes me feel this way
and that's the truth
the only one
I know

THE HAPPY ENDING

sometimes life can seem especially dark

but

at the end of the day

we all want to believe

in fairytales

and magic

we all hope and pray

that the whispered rumors of mystical truths ring true

and hold hope in our foolish hearts

the happy ending exists

ACKNOWLEDGMENTS

I am an emotional creature.

I feel everything very deeply, and for a long time I saw this as a weakness.

Thank you to all the badass women and individuals who support and encourage me to embrace every aspect of my most authentic self.

This book wouldn't exist without you.

Thank you, Cleo, Danielle, Bianca, and innumerable others for guiding me toward this end result.

Thank you, Nora, for your endless enthusiasm.

And lastly, thank YOU for reading these words.

I love you.

Thank you for feeling with me.

xx

www.ingramcontent.com/pod-product-compliance
Lightning Source LLC
Chambersburg PA
CBHW021623270326
41931CB00008B/845